A House

by Ethan Flores
illustrated by Marianne Tanner

Practice Pre-Decodable 3

McGraw Hill Education

Bothell, WA • Chicago, IL • Columbus, OH • New York, NY

MHEonline.com

Send all inquiries to:
McGraw-Hill Education
8787 Orion Place
Columbus, OH 43240

ISBN: 978-0-02-132202-2
MHID: 0-02-132202-3

Printed in the United States of America.

8 9 10 CTM 23

a 

truck

a 

hammer

a 

saw

a 

ladder

a 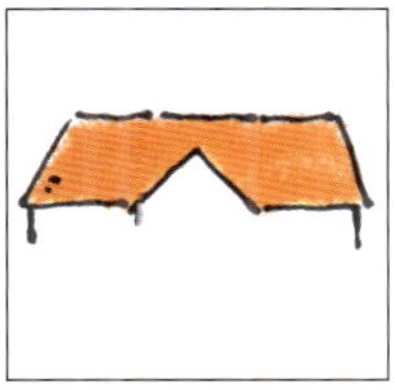

roof

a 

key